THE GRANDPARENTS RECORD BOOK

ALAN HUTCHISON PUBLISHING CO. LTD.

THE FIRST GRANDCHILD

Name John Jacques

Birth date 27th September 1995

Birth place Lakeshore General Hospital

Birth weight 8 lbs 8 ozs

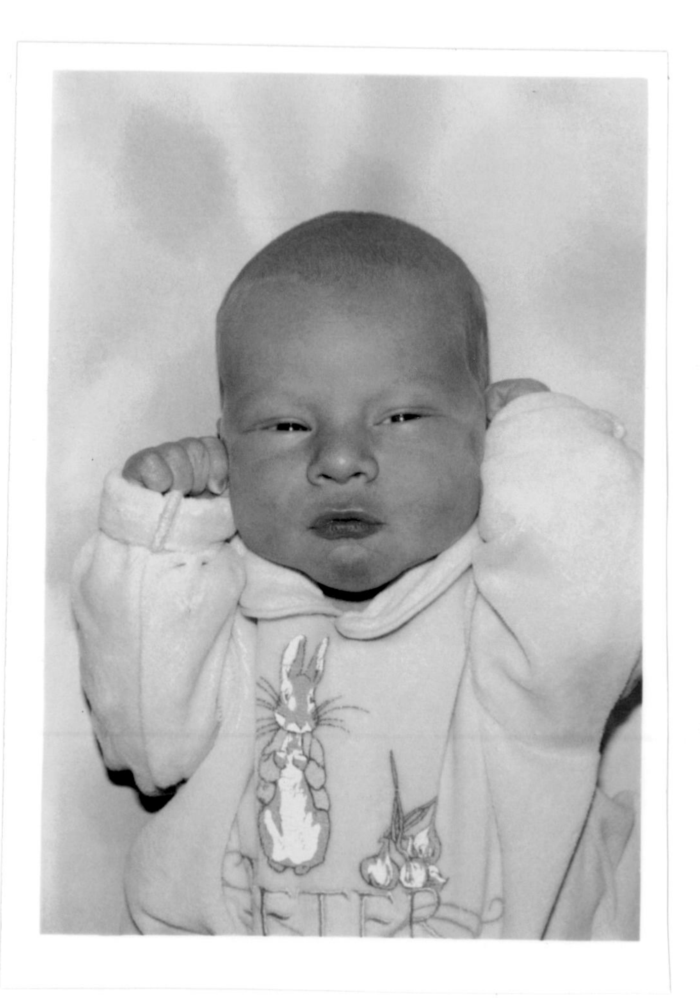

THE VISIT TO THE NURSERY (detail)
Jean-Honoré Fragonard (1732-1806)
Samuel H Kress Collection

THE 2nd GRANDCHILD

Name RHYS ANDREW

Birth date 27th October 1997

Birth place Lakeshore General Hospital

Birth weight 8 lbs 9 ozs

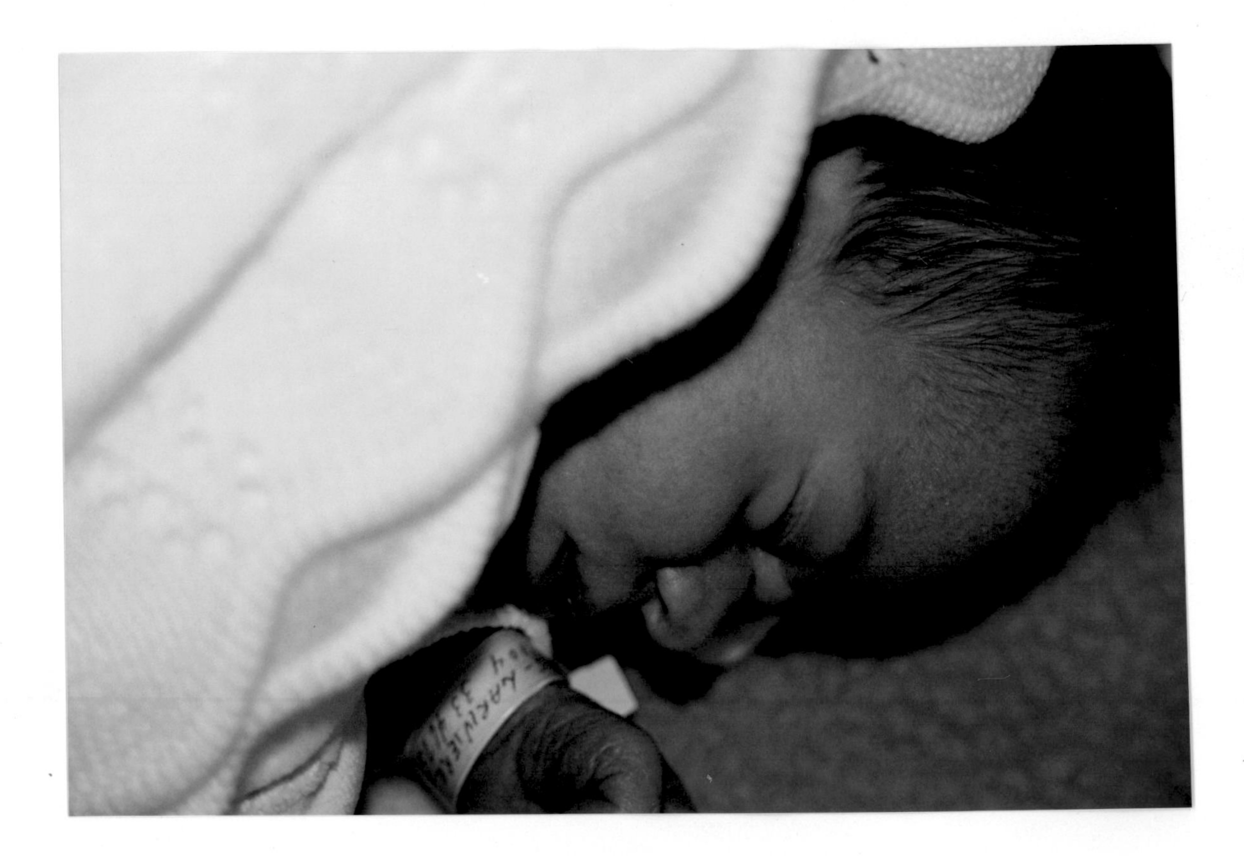

THE GRANDCHILD

Name ....

Birth date ....

Birth place ....

Birth weight ....

THE GRANDCHILD

Name ....

Birth date ....

Birth place ....

Birth weight ....

THE GRANDCHILD

Name ....

Birth date ....

Birth place ....

Birth weight ....

THE SLEEPING BABE
Rudolf Epp (1878-1939)

The Grandchild

Name ....

Birth date ....

Birth place ....

Birth weight ....

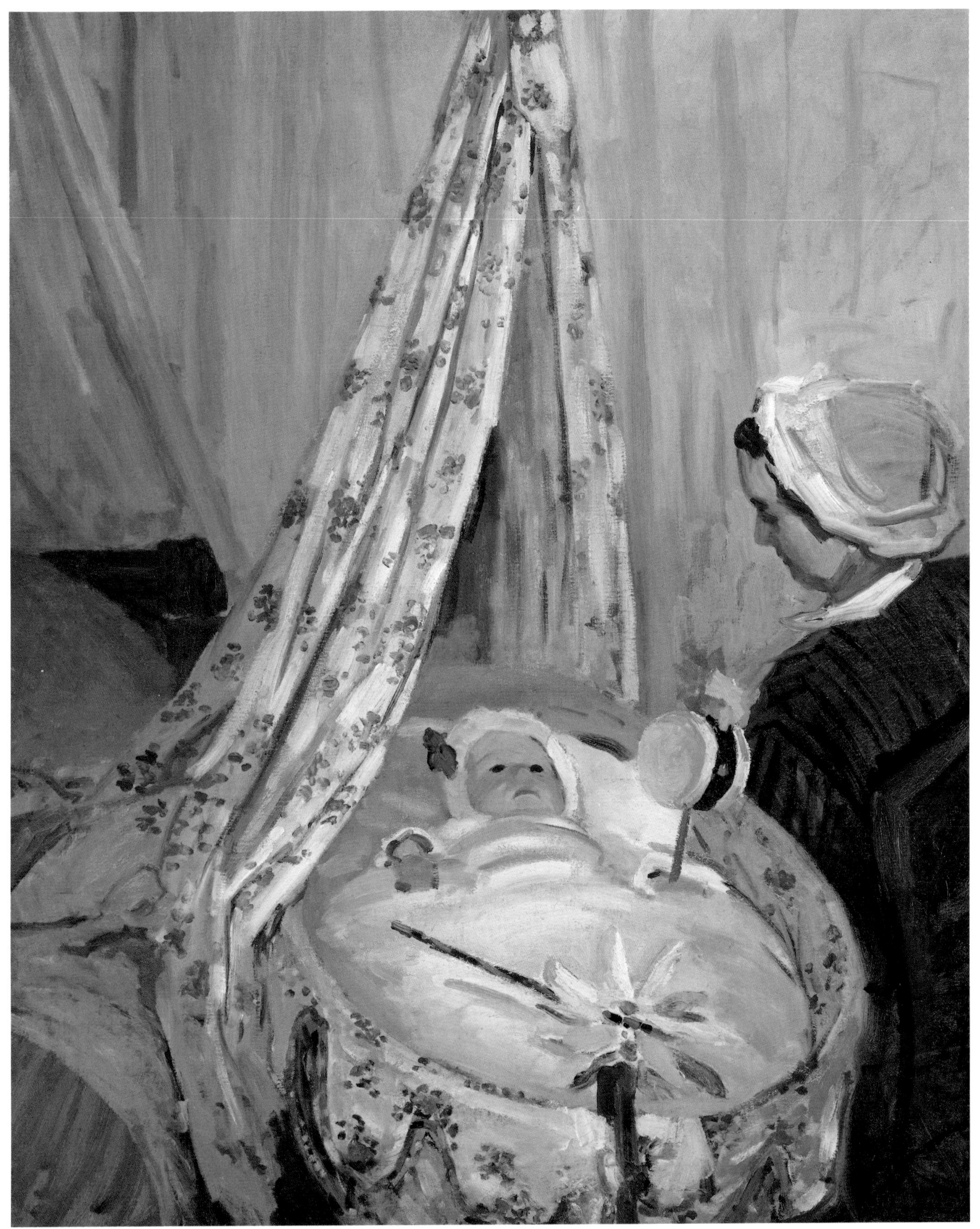

THE CRADLE – CAMILLE WITH THE ARTIST'S SON, JEAN
Claude Monet (1840-1926)
Collection of Mr and Mrs Paul Mellon

THE GRANDCHILD

Name ....

Birth date ....

Birth place ....

Birth weight ....

REMARKS

THE CHRISTENING OF THE FIRST GRANDCHILD

John Jacques

Christened 14th April 1996 at St Thomas More Church
Verdun

By Reverend George S. Oakes

Godparents. Michael Davies – (Uncle)
Paul Church
Jacqueline Morasco – (aunt)

Many friends and family present, John Jacques received many lovely gifts.

The day started with a snowstorm but by evening the sun was shining.

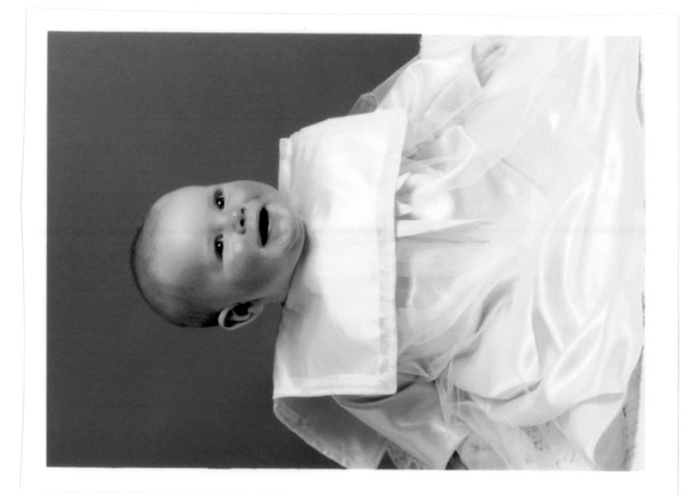

CHRISTENING SUNDAY
James Charles (1851-1906)

THE CHRISTENING OF THE SECOND GRANDCHILD

July 11th 1998. I'm not able to join them but will be there in thought

Godparents Laurie Descoteaux (aunt)
Danny Lariviere (uncle

THE CHRISTENING OF THE GRANDCHILD

PETROGRAD

Petror Vodkin (1878-1939)

The Christening Of The Grandchild

The Christening Of The Grandchild

The Christening Of The Grandchild

MATERNAL KISS
Mary Cassatt (1844-1926)
Bequest of Anne Huichman

The Christening Of The .... Grandchild

Remarks

GRANDCHILDREN'S BIRTHDAY

First grandchild's first birthday

Name John Jacques (J.J.)

Telephoned on JJ's birthday, spoke to him & tried to make animal noises over the phone, sadly he doesn't know me or my voice but hopefully one day that will all change. Sent Toys R Us vouchers for his birthday, they were used to buy a tricycle & some other small gifts.

1997 – 2nd Birthday. Sent money for present, – a basket-ball game, clothes and a computer game. Phoned and spoke with JJ, he chats quite well now.

1998 – 3rd Birthday. Sent money for Andrew & Jeannie to buy JJ a bike – little red one with stabliser wheels, enough cash to also buy him a "Spiderman motorcycle" !! I was in Italy for his birthday but have received photos showing he really likes his bike

1999 – 4th Birthday. I am with the family to enjoy the occassion – big party, all the children from his class at nursery school & children of family + friends as well. I bought him a racing car set amongst other things – I think it made me laugh more than J.J.

BABY'S BIRTHDAY

Frederick Daniel Hardy (1826-1911)

GRANDCHILDREN'S BIRTHDAY

Name Rhys Andrew

Age 1 year (Oct 1998)

Sent money for Andrew + Jeannie to buy him presents. Received photographs of his party – he's a big lad, I'll be seeing him soon – at Christmas.

Oct 1999 – 2nd Birthday, bought his presents + left them with Andrew + Jeannie as I arrived home before the 24th. He did unpack one gift – the little train/funfair – it was nice to see him enjoy it.

Oct 2000 3rd Birthday. Our Rhys is growing fast can't be with him this birthday but I'll be thinking of him, such a handsome affectionate little one.

Grandchildren's Birthday

Name ....

Age ....

HERE'S GRANNY
George Smith (1829-1901)

Grandchildren's Birthday

Name John Jacques

Age 5 years

Sept 2000 J.J. is starting full time school now, he attends a French school and is doing so well.

Grandchildren's Birthday

Name ....

Age ....

Grandchildren's Birthday

Name ....

Age ....

EUGÈNE MANET AND HIS DAUGHTER IN THE GARDEN AT BOUGIVAL (DETAIL)

Berthe Morisot (1841-1895) Private Collection

Grandchildren's Birthday

Name ....

Age ....

Photographs

REMARKS

March 2nd 2001 J.J. to have his tonsils + adenoids removed.

TIME FLIES
William G. Barry (fl. 1888)

VISITS TO GRANDCHILDREN

First visit to J.J. Oct 1st 1995, mother and baby just home from hospital – such a beautiful baby boy. Returned to England Oct 15th with my foot in plaster.

Michael & I went to Canada April 4th 1996 to see JJ & his Mum & Dad and to be present at his Christening on April 14th.

May 1997 spent 10 days with the family. J.J. is growing so tall, seems more than 18 mths old, very lively. loves the park swings. Eats really well – in fact he's just about perfect!!

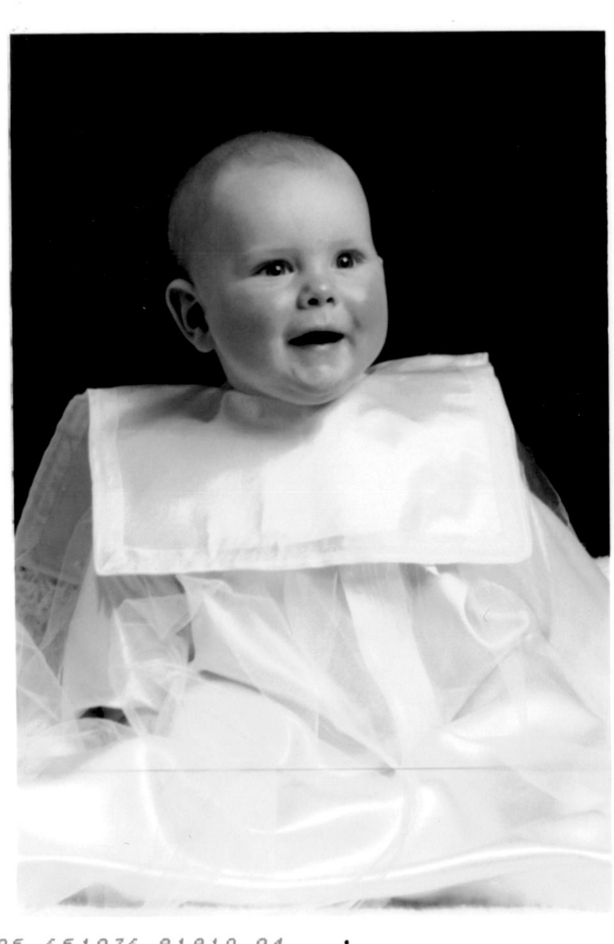

THE THORN
James Hallyar (1829-1920)

VISITS TO GRANDCHILDREN

December 29th 1997.

The first time to see Rhys – another beautiful grandson. I think he's going to be a big boy. 2 months old and he has a wonderful smile – good lungs too when he's hungry!!

J.J. is growing up – adorable boy, crazy about ice hockey.

Serious ice storm beginning of January causing power cuts and many problems. Thankful Jeannie is feeding Rhys or difficulties would be even greater.

Rhys Andrew
3½ months.

VISITS TO GRANDCHILDREN

Sept/Oct 1999 In Montreal for J.J.'s 4th Birthday, such lovely kids, shame we are so far apart

February 2000

In Montreal to help Jeannie, she is bedridden after having operations on both feet & Andrew had to go to L.A on business. Lots of snow, J.J inclined to get a bit upset, naturally it must seem very strange to him. Rhys is younger & not a care in the world.

June 2001

Such a joy to see the boys, they met me at the airport with flowers, I'll always remember J J's face as he came towards me holding the roses. They both seem happy to see me & we had a lot of fun.

Oct 2002

Visiting this time to be with family for Rhys' 5th birthday, J.J is 7 now both are growing up so fast. They both have lots of interests now. As their birthdays are quite close (1 month apart) I bought them a PlayStation 2 between them. Both boys were able to play the games etc so quickly & seemed to really enjoy it — so did their Dad!!

VISITS TO GRANDCHILDREN

Christmas 2004.

My first Christmas in Canada - deep snow, very cold but so beautiful - like a Christmas card world. Had a really wonderful time, the boys seemed to have changed a lot since they were here in the summer, both very much into ice hockey, so glad I was able to see them both playing. Visited their school for the Christmas shows, J.J's year was far & away the most successful, he looked great in his costume - got a picture & a mention in the local paper. The ice was so thick they were able to skate on the drive.

The HRS Atom B Ice Dogs were finalists in the Tournoi Christian-Bourbonnais in St. Polycarpe this past week-end. They were undefeated going into their final game against La Petite Nation but unfortunately lost in overtime 7-6. It was an amazing day for Gabriel Gaudette who got 5 goals for the Ice Dogs. All the kids played extremely well and were thrilled with their medals as well as the Finalist banner they received, which will be signed by all players and fly proudly at Bourget Arena in Rigaud.

Dec 2004

Travelling through time

by ERIN METCALFE

The halls at St. Thomas Elementary School were filled last week with students and parents touring the Époque Open House, offering a travel through time from the prehistoric ages in the kindergarten section to contemporary times in the Grade 6 classes.

Hudson

Photo Erin Metcalfe

Posed behind a crafty rendition of "les seigneuries en 1745" and wearing the costumes to match are, above, Grade 4 students John-Jacques Davies, Lara-Maria Breton and Mathieu Masse with their teacher, Rachel Quesnel.

The ***Hudson Gazette*** was priviledged to have a guided tour of each class, led informatively by two knowledgable and gracious Grade 6 students, Nicholas Boudreau and Samuel Breton.

In the prehistoric era, the kindergarten students, costumed in brown paper as cavemen, pointed to their very own cave drawings and their display of primitive tools and fur skins.

Upstairs the Grade 2 classes had impressive presentations to give about about the Egyptian era, including explanations about pyramids and treasures. A special treat was another Grade 2 class that sang and played their projects about the Renaissance period were expertly displayed by Grade 3 classes and their previously video-taped rendition of a renaissance circus pleased many onlookers.

This led into the Grade 4 presentations of La Nouvelle France, with fabulously designed costumes in which one could easily have felt lost in time! Each student gave remarkable presentations of their paired projects,

It continued. Through the Middle Ages with coats of arms designed by daycare students up to the Grade 5 classes giving informative and creative presentations on the Romantic era.

Grade 6 classes were full of information about World Wars 1 and ll, about the technology and evolution of bombs, about the culture of the 60's, and even the social- economic trends between the 1960s and 1990s.

Visits From Grandchildren

J. J's first visit December 9th 1995 to January 5th 1996

December 1995

THE COTTAGE HOME (DETAIL)

William H. Snape (active 1885-1892)

VISITS FROM GRANDCHILDREN

December 1998

J.J. & Rhys were here with me for Christmas, so lovely to see them & get to know them properly. J.J is growing up fast, so interesting now. Rhys is an adorable little monkey!!

VISITS FROM GRANDCHILDREN

December 2001 – January 7th 2002

J. J + Rhys came for Christmas + New Year. It was a great visit – boys loved their presents. Rhys was so good when his truck refused to work on Christmas morning, I think I was most disappointed. Andrew + Rhys arrived four days before J. J + Jeannie, it was a lovely opportunity to really get to know him. Played games + went to the park, visit to "Jolly Roger" was a great success. J. J was with us for the second visit to "Jolly Roger – he loved it. We all went to the pantomime, J. J's enjoyment was a real joy to see; Rhys was a bit dubious until the "ghost" came on then he yelled with the best!! They both got on well with Jamie + Stephanie – nice for them all.

BLIND MAN'S BUFF

Frederick Morgan (1856-1927)

VISITS FROM GRANDCHILDREN

June/July 2004

Family here for Michael's 50th Birthday celebration etc.

Andrew + Jeannie went to Scotland for 4/5 days, boys stayed with me, we went out a lot during those days. Visits to Jolly Roger (firm favourite) Bowood Adventure playground, Bibury Trout farm and Paultons Theme Park, Sam joined us with Stephie + Jamie.

They returned to Canada July 9th + took Jamie with them to spend the school summer holidays in Montreal.

THE ARTIST'S GARDEN AT VETHEUIL

Claude Monet (1840-1926)

Alisa Mellon Bruce Collection

Family Holidays and Outings

Photographs

MOTHER AND DAUGHTER, BOTH WEARING LARGE HATS

Mary Cassatt (1844-1926)

Family Holidays and Outings

Photographs

Family Holidays and Outings

THE APPLE HARVEST

Carl Larsson (1853-1919)

Family Holidays and Outings

Photographs

Family Holidays and Outings

SUMMERTIME IN GLOUCESTERSHIRE
James Archer (1822-1904)

Special Occasions

THE ARBOUR (DETAIL)

E. Phillips Fox (1864-1915)

Special Occasions

Special Occasions

THE CAULD BLAST
Joshua Hargrave Mann (fl. 1849-1884)

Presents for Grandchildren

Have started an investment for JJ to mature for him on his 18th birthday. Invesco Rupert Children's fund. Hope he will use it usefully but to give him pleasure – that's what presents are for.

Have given him a £1000 Bond, this will mature on his 21st birthday – have fun my love.

J.J's Christening gift – a gold St. Christopher medallion.

Have started an investment fund for Rhys – same as JJ's it will mature on his 18th birthday, also given him a National Savings Bond £1000 this will mature on his 21st birthday. Hope he will enjoy the proceeds of both and know that I was thinking of him with love.

Rhys' Christening gift – gold St. Christopher engraved with his name + Christening date

CARNATION, LILY, LILY AND ROSE
John Singer Sargent (1856-1925)

Presents for Grandchildren

PRESENTS FOR GRANDCHILDREN

BRETON GIRLS DANCING, PONT AVEN
Paul Gauguin (1848-1903)
Collection of Mr and Mrs Paul Mellon

Presents for Grandchildren

PRESENTS FOR GRANDCHILDREN

THE CHIMNEY CORNER
Joseph Clark (1834-1926)

Presents From Grandchildren

Tricycle with basket of dried flowers Jan 96
arrived after JJ and family went home.

J. J. made me table mats and a photograph
frame for Christmas 98 – I shall always
treasure them.

Lovely serviettes from boys for Christmas 2001. also beautiful
photographs of them both + another tree decoration to add to
my collection.

Christmas 2002 – great collection of C.D's from the
family

JEAN, JEANNE AND JEANETTE
Elizabeth Adela Forbes (1859-1912)

Presents From Grandchildren

PRESENTS FROM GRANDCHILDREN

PICKING FLOWERS
Dorothea Sharp (1874-1955)

GRANDCHILDREN'S EARLY ACHIEVEMENTS

J.J's first steps at 10 months

Walking well by 1st Birthday – (10 teeth)

Can write his initials (J.J) at 2 years

Rhys first step 9½ months. Walking well at 11 mths

Rhys starting to talk at 18 months

J.J's first school report – very good

April 2001 2nd report – all Grade I he's doing so well

Another excellent report card for J.J. first one in his new school, he's done so well & his French is already very fluent for his age.

J J's School reports continue to be very good, Rhys not yet in school, his birthday falls outside the annual catchment area but his pre-school teacher obviously thinks so much of him + his young friends all love him – guess he's the most popular young pupil – they say he makes them laugh, well in my book that's a great gift, he really is a joyful little boy.

THE MUSIC LESSON

Lord Frederick Leighton (1830-1896)

Grandchildren's Early Achievements

Grandchildren's Early Achievements

BO PEEP (PEEK A BOO)
Eastman Johnson (1824-1906)

Grandchildren's Early Achievements

MADAME MONET AND HER SON (detail)
Auguste Renoir (1841-1919)
Alisa Mellon Bruce Collection

Grandchildren's Early Achievements

GRANDCHILDREN'S EARLY ACHIEVEMENTS

TRY THIS PAIR

Frederick Daniel Hardy (1826-1911)

Grandmother's Advice for the Future

THE POPPY GATHERER
David Fulton (1848-1930)

Grandmother's Advice For The Future

GRANDMOTHER'S ADVICE FOR THE FUTURE

IDLE HOURS
William Merritt Chase (1849-1916)

Grandfather's Advice For The Future

PORTRAIT OF THE ARTIST'S SON TITUS

Harmensz Van Rijn Rembrandt (1606-1669)

Grandfather's Advice for the Future

Grandfather's Advice For The Future

JAMES WYATT AND HIS GRANDDAUGHTER
John Everett Millais (1829-1896)

COVER:

THE ARBOUR (DETAIL)

E. Phillips Fox (1864-1915)

FRONTISPIECE:

SUNDAY MORNING – THE WALK FROM CHURCH

Richard Redgrave (1804-1888) Private Collection

The Publishers are very grateful to the following organisations, individuals and institutions for their kind permission to reproduce their pictures:

Amon Carter Museum, Fort Worth, USA; Bridgeman Art Library; Christies Colour Library; Christopher Wood Gallery; Crawford Municipal Gallery, Cork, Eire; Guildhall Art Gallery, London; Manchester City Art Gallery; The National Gallery of Art, Washington, USA; National Gallery of Victoria, Australia; National Gallery of Scotland; The Norton Simon Foundation; The Philadelphia Museum of Art; Phillips Fine Art Auctioneers; Photographie Giraudon; The Royal Holloway Collection; Roy Miles Fine Paintings; Society of Cultural Relations with USSR; The Tate Gallery; The Wolverhampton Art Gallery.

Published by Alan Hutchison Publishing Co
9 Pembridge Studios
27a Pembridge Villas
London W11 3EP

Worldwide distribution

HELPING THE ENVIRONMENT

All the pages of this book are made from woodfree products (plant fibres, rags, grass etc). The cover boards contain low grade particles of renewable soft wood.

Printed and bound in Hong Kong

ISBN 185 272 9732